Write to be Read, Speak to be Heard

a communication guide
to the 5 Filters

DAYNA E. MAZZUCA

ISBN-13: 978-0-9950108-6-4

*Between us a word... to speak
and be heard.*

TABLE OF CONTENTS

INTRODUCTION

If you speak to be heard—or write to be read—then you know people wear filters.

When someone filters our words, they make choices to invite us in—or keep us out—of their mental, emotional and spiritual landscape. These decisions happen in a blink. They are invisible to our eye, yet we know they exist and that they matter.

We know what it means to be heard, to have someone receive what we say. To be heard is one of life's great joys. It's powerful and often transformative. But we also know what it means to miss the mark, to have someone resist what we say. To walk away. To close the book. In this case, we're often left wondering what went wrong: to imagine what we might have said or done differently. If only we'd known…

Filters play a vital and dynamic role in how people hear us, or not. From an aspiring communicator's point of view, filters are first-gate issues. They are too important to ignore. They may be invisible, but they don't have to be inscrutable. We can take a close and revealing look at how others may be receiving or rejecting our words. We can explore the filters people wear. We can work to be heard by becoming aware of the role and needs of these filters. And learn how to accommodate them without compromising the meat of our words. There is no use speaking if no one's listening. And I'd suggest there's little point unless—and until—we have our listener's fuller attention. Not all readers or listeners lend both ears to what they read, but unless someone is offering what they have capacity to offer, why bother? Why waste our words on ears slanted in an entirely different direction, attuned to another conversation?

If someone's having a conversation in their own head while we're speaking and seeking to be heard, then I'm thinking it's important to tap into that primary conversation, to align with the inner monologue someone's hosting while we assume they're listening to us, just because their eyes are on us. People hear with their ears. And their minds. And their hearts. The conversation is complex and multi-faceted. There's a lot going on in the simple exchange—and hope—of writing to be read or speaking to be heard.

We can speak to be heard and write to be read. We just need to be aware of our listener as a fuller participant, realizing they have an important role to play in what we say. Speaking with the best intentions is no guarantee those intentions are clear. Not to anyone. Our listener plays an active role in interpreting, synthesizing, accepting or rejecting our words. This is true whether we speak from the stage, pulpit, platform or on the page or through the screen. Communication is a dynamic, as opposed to a cliched, two-way street.

People are not passive, ensuring no conversation is pure monologue. And that's a great thing. The speaking and listening process is not static; it's relational. This means our words have the potential to form real bonds of understanding, enlightenment, respect and intimacy between us and our listener or reader.

People are not machines and the act of communication is not mechanical. It's the lifeblood of any community. The source of learning. The power to change. The reason to get up in the morning. And the door to truth.

There's always someone on the other side of what we say, waiting to hear, receive, be blessed by our words. Moved by our intent. Touched by our content, inspired by our ideas. What we say matters; but how our reader receives what we say matters more.

A song must be heard to be
complete.
Danny MacDonald, East Coast
musician

We can speak to be heard and write to be read. With some time and effort, we can understand how people filter our words, exactly. Once we recognize these filters, we can be proactive and adjust to accommodate them. We can even appreciate the role they play in ensuring our communication stays relational and has real impact. As long as our words are authentic and ring true to who we are, we have an excellent chance of reaching our audience.

This book is about the Five Filters that represent Five Types of Readers—the Scholar, Social Connector, Change Agent, Adventurer and Mystic—whom you may recognize in your own life, but be new to you as readers.

Each type of reader has their own set of questions, needs and expectations. While these filters also play a key role in spontaneous, interpersonal communication, this book focuses on more intentional acts such as writing for an audience or speaking to a public.

This book is about recognizing which type of reader you're best equipped to reach, according to your own set of filters—and empowering you to reach them on a more effectual and meaningful level. It's about improving your communication with your type of reader. It's about writing to be read and speaking to be heard.

FIVE FILTERS
FIVE TYPES OF READERS

Meet the SCHOLAR

This type is the resident expert in the room.

The Scholar is demanding, but respectful. They give more than they take. Anyone wearing this reader's filter loves to learn and share what they know. They spend a lot of time in their head—solving problems, answering questions and generally building a better world through a solid base of knowledge and know-how. They filter what you say through your ability to engage them intellectually and love to be in conversation with stimulating thinkers.

The informed imagination also plays a strong filtering role for this reader. Your ability to connect the dots and flesh out possibilities puts you in good with the Scholar. They may be the resident expert, but there's always room for one more great idea. Knowledge, by definition, is meant to be shared. This reader does not read in isolation. They're aware of those who have come before and give credit where credit is due. They take a layered, contextual view of the world and appreciate those who do the same.

If you like to work with ideas and understand their source and future potential, this may be your type of reader.

QUESTIONS
When wearing this filter, this reader is asking themselves, "Is this person trustworthy? Are they credible? Should I invest time and energy to hear more? Do they have something to teach?"

Because this reader is usually well-informed, they tend to trust their own instinct when making this kind of judgement call.

This is not a reflection on you, the writer or speaker. This type is simply committed to conserving and managing their mental energy. They won't engage unless there's some overlap between what you say and what they already know and are processing in their own head.

There has to be a point of intellectual or imaginative connectivity for them to hear you. It's impossible to speak to this listener from out of the blue. Context is key. You must speak from a position of shared knowledge and understanding of the world.

The Scholar must sense some return on their intellectual investment in order to receive and engage with what you have to say.

EXPECTATIONS
The writer who connects with this reader is a natural teacher—the facts don't have to be new, if the observations are fresh and stimulating. This reader expects the writer to have a command of his or her material and present it masterfully.

The Scholar is the high-wire acrobat, seeking unique and daring viewpoints, without losing sight of basic safety rules and measures. This is someone who gets excited about possibilities. Loves to discuss ideas! This reader has little tolerance for people they find boring. It's too important for them to maintain their mental edge and alertness. Up there on the wire.

*Repeating the obvious will only bore
and irritate the Scholar. They seek
and need high-wire stimuli.*

This reader demands accurate, stimulating writing. Aim high, but do not muddle things. Blurry lines, confused or lazy thinking does not sit well with this type. They demand clarity, focus and not a little fortitude and panache.

IF THIS IS YOUR READER
If this is your type of reader, ideas and insights come naturally to you. You are quick to credit sources and willing to establish your own credibility. You are known for getting the facts straight. Your communication is typically respectful and solidly structured. Your content valuable. You are that rare animal: an informed risk-taker. You're willing to push limits and go places others hardly dream of going.

You have a deep regard for your would-be audience. You generally succeed in communicating with the Scholars in the room, sharing a mutual trust and admiration for how to filter words.

Meet the SOCIAL CONNECTOR

The Social Connector serves to foster community and strengthen ties within their circle of influence. They are skillful jugglers of peoples' needs and demands. The Connector is the hub of their circle. At the heart of their life and work are the people they know and love—and the projects that keep life interesting.

This means they filter communication through a criterium of personal relevancy. If what you have to say doesn't speak to the circle, this type will struggle to hear you. They have only so much energy and need to direct it towards what serves and benefits the community.

Life is not theoretical or conceptual. It is practical, personal and full of problems. They don't need to trust your credentials; they need to trust your heart, to know you come from a place of empathy for the human condition. They need to know you're safe before they know you're smart.

The Connector is not on the high-wire performing elite feats; they are filling the stands and leading the cheer from the ground. But before they can applaud your accomplishments or achievements, they need to know your name, something about you. Something personal. For this type, familiarity trumps fame.

If you value people's personal stories and prioritize the needs of the community, this may be your type of reader.

QUESTIONS

While deciding to pay attention to what you say, or politely shut you out, the Social Connector is asking, "How does this relate to my situation? How can I apply this? Does it speak to me and mine?"

These are not selfish questions. They are necessary. This reader, while giving themselves fully to the people and projects in their lives, works hard not to overextend themselves. They tend to live at personal capacity, or slightly beyond it. Relevancy becomes the litmus test for what this reader can receive and what they must reject.

If what you have to say isn't relevant and/or applicable, they won't take from Peter to give to Paul. What you say needs immediacy and intimacy. Connectors favour the friendly and familiar.

EXPECTATIONS

Who doesn't like a good story? Story is human. Although, for this reader, narrative is the norm. They think, live and act from a story point of view. People take on voices. Dialogue fills the air. Personalities become characters in the ongoing drama of life. Homes and offices take on descriptive qualities reminiscent of stage settings. They appreciate the power of story. Charts, visuals and diagrams—which speak to the other four types—fall short of the mark for this reader. Without a good story, this reader proves slightly hard of hearing.

A good story makes for a good day.

IF THIS IS YOUR READER
If this is your reader, you are a storyteller. You understand the power of empathy; the underlying motivations that drive people; the situations we all face.

You speak from within the circle, not beyond the pale.

Your language is inclusive, invitational and intimate. You do not fear feelings. The life of the heart—where people really live—is central to your understanding of the world. There's no such thing as earning the right to be heard. It is a birthright. And life is best lived out loud, together, serving the common. One shared problem at a time.

If this is your reader, you validate the universal longing for acceptance. "I believe in you," is your constant theme.

Meet the CHANGE AGENT

The Change Agent is on a mission. They are an inspiring force for good. Big picture thinkers. They filter what they hear according to the causes they support, rather than the people they call their own. They are real-world, pragmatic idealists. They respond to the language of passion rather than empathy. They see potential, not problems.

> *A man's reach should exceed his grasp, or what's a heaven for? –*
> *Robert Browning, poet*

They seek to help those who cannot help themselves, often by righting the wrongs that created the situation in the first place. While working on team to address societal issues, this type is motivated to serve the marginalized, invisible and persecuted. Although unwilling to sit long with a problem or an individual, they are moved by compassion and see a direct link between the work they do and the people groups who stand to benefit.

This means they filter what they hear through a lens of causality rather than connectivity. They're not listening for intellectual overlap, or familiar voices speaking on friendly topics. They're listening to get involved, to act justly. To make a difference.

This reader seeks to be inspired and impassioned.

They are looking to do good work, better. To be empowered rather than educated or encouraged. This is an action-oriented reader.

If you have a passion for making the world a better place, one great project at a time, this may be your reader.

QUESTIONS

As you speak, this reader is asking themselves, "Is this person worth reckoning with; do they have energy to harness; passion to harvest?"

These are not cold, impersonal questions. They are ways of assessing alignment. Does what you say help move their cause(s) forward? Do you bring passion to the table? Can you help them help others?

The ability to move things forward is a biggie for this reader. Change means moving forward. Not staying stuck. Resisting status quo. Life is not a circle, it's a battlefront.

Energy and focus are key.

The Change Agent is not seeking the spotlight. They're not on the high wire performing daring acts. They're not in the stands, enjoying the show and adding laughter to people's day. They are the ringmasters. They make sure the show goes on and goes on for all. They are the ones calling out to the people in the street, the alleys, to come and see something new and exciting. Something to bring crowds to their feet! Something worth applauding.

EXPECTATIONS
Short. Succinct. To the point.

Next!

This is what the Change Agent expects. Someone who knows what they're talking about and says it effectively. Someone who understands time is short and the issues urgent. They appreciate communicators who don't indulge in leisurely stories that ramble and ideas that tend to morph. To reach the Change Agent you need focus on clarity and emphasize the consequence of your words.

IF THIS IS YOUR READER
If this is your reader, you are a concept person who also values results. You are committed to what you promote. You don't apologize for taking a stand on issues that cut close to the bone. You believe in the unlimited potential of team effort, and back these efforts as long as the end goal is worthy and the destination clear.

You don't expect your reader to always agree or align with you. Although, like the Change Agent, you know that agreement and alignment are two bright green lights on the road to change.

Meet the ADVENTURER

The Adventurer is a friend to anyone with a mountain to climb, physical or otherwise. They feel most alive when facing a challenge head-on, coming alongside someone they care about. When the summit of success is in sight, almost. It's that gap between where we are now and where we could be that the Adventurer longs to close.

This reader is not about addressing injustice or societal wrongs. They ache for people to experience a personal-to-them victory, straddle their own mountaintop. This reader understands the restorative, reclaiming power of overcoming. They know most obstacles are personal. And that people do better when greatness is in reach.

This type despises the attitude and language of self-defeat.

The Adventurer is not seeking to change the world, only broaden perspective, to lend courage. This type knows what it means to live with hope, vision and dreams. And they sense the catastrophe of living without them. They filter what they hear according to its ability to dignify and embolden the soul.

Life is not a perpetual to-do list; it's a one-of-a-kind mountain to master.

QUESTIONS
As you speak, the Adventurer asks, "Is courage required? Am I needed? Wanted?"

Like the Change Agent, this is an action-oriented reader. They seek to participate, even vicariously while sprawled long on the sofa, in the adventure of living life full-on.

This reader is not without their philosophies, however. They understand that the joy of climbing the mountain depends on who's on the trek. Emotional fitness is part of their makeup, alongside physical finesse and endurance. They love to draw on this capacity for courage, to help others grow strong. Fight the good fight.

They do not aim to connect with many, but with a few hardy souls willing to give life a go. This means they respond to the language of individualism as well as close relationship. It means they read a lot to glean a lot. They are committed to being found prepared; ready to risk for one in need. To be a hands-on friend in times of trouble.

They're not seeking to be empowered, only equipped. They do not need you to persuade them, only prompt. To point them towards the mountain top. To allow them to become immersed in the challenge at hand.

EXPECTATIONS
The mountain matters. Life matters. Human encounters with obstacles that threaten to overwhelm carry weight. Endurance has worth. And courage is everything.

This means the Adventurer expects you to give it your all. Do not hold back.

Immerse, immerse, immerse.

Believability is essential. They are listening for the voice of someone's who's been there, done that. Someone who knows how to keep a story moving through the use of selective detail. This reader hates to get bogged down. At the same time, they're quick to spot the gaps and untenable leaps in a story.

At base, this reader is looking for a grace-filled, hard-won perspective. They know you can't climb a mountain, stand on the summit, look out over infinity and come back the same. Taking on life's challenges changes a person, for the better. Wading in the shallows, mucking over disappointments, does not nurture this reader and will not sustain their interest. The burden of doubt has no cache with the Adventurer. This reader is a believer in the best life and its human participants have to offer.

There must be a sense of "this is real." And "it matters."

IF THIS IS YOUR READER
If your horizons stretch past life's difficulties and towards its summits, this may be your reader. Chances are, you already know a few. Adventurers are good at converging according to strength and ability. They watch people; see the way they carry themselves; assess if they speak from a place of experience. If this is your reader, you share a creed of overcoming. You give your best and look for the same in others.

Meet the MYSTIC

The Mystic is the poet listening for spiritual intimations that speak to the truth they live. They strive to expand on the vault of revelation in the world, to add a word of life where they can. To bless others by staying true to themselves, living by faith to the best of their ability. They are pilgrims. The Mystic calls a larger, unseen reality—the spiritual plane of life—their true home and destination.

If what you say speaks to the ineffable side of life, this may be your reader.

When you speak to the Mystic, only a few words are usually needed to get their attention. This reader is not a consumer of words and images; they don't read for information or entertainment. They read to grow and understand, adding to their own core convictions. The Mystic brings much to the conversation, even as they maintain silence.

When they do choose to listen, they are excellent listeners, attentive to and appreciative of deep, human-held, divinely inspired connections.

Deep calls to deep. Psalm 42:7

QUESTIONS
When discerning whether or not to listen closely to you, the Mystic asks, "Does this ring true? Does it align with my core beliefs? Witness with my spirit, resonate with my

soul?" These are highly subjective questions—ones not easily answered.

In many ways, the Mystic is an audience of one.

The answer to their questions depends on their alignment with your words, tone and intent. The Mystic is seeking unity, to apprehend reality by the lights of the truth they hold dear. A truth that is timeless. The Mystic longs to dwell in eternity here and now. This means the timeliness of what you say—its prophetic quality and spiritual resonance—matters.

The Mystic desires to commune with the divine.

They are asking themselves if what you have to say will bring them closer to God.

EXPECTATIONS
The Mystic is a reflective reader. They require a level of intimacy in order to hear you. A breathability and authenticity behind and within your words. A certain fearlessness with the truth. There's no way to fudge the facts or embellish a story to the point of believability with a Mystic. They've spent a lifetime cultivating the gift of discernment. And they don't make apologies for how they navigate the world or make decisions.

The Mystic likes to ponder the felt, but unseen side of life. To apprehend the wonders of God. The language of metaphor is one they know well.

They don't expect you to have all the answers. They'd rather discover those themselves. They do, however, appreciate those who foster an atmosphere of inquiry and depth; who invite others to ask good questions.

IF THIS IS YOUR READER

If this is your reader, you are already in conversation with them. You share their language and appreciate the prophetic, inexpressible side of life. You are not afraid to speak your truth: to own and live it. And, you are quick to offer the kind of assurance the Mystic needs to hear: "I recognize and respect you." You are a fellow bridge builder between the heights of heaven and the stuff of earth. You love to dwell on deep truths and take care in how you communicate with others.

THESE ARE THE 5 FILTERS, in brief.

Ideally you recognized some of your own filtering-work and the type(s) of reader you want to reach with your words. You may choose to focus on one type and write to them to go deep. Or you may need to reach a broader audience—to go wide. We speak differently to a small gathering than with a larger one.

If you have the luxury to focus on one type of reader, you can indulge their needs and preferences; forge a strong, sympathetic bond by accommodating all their filters. In this case, your words will have depth, but lack range. You will be limited to reaching one or two types effectively.

If you need to reach all five types, you have to meet the basic requirements of each kind of listener in your ideal audience. Your words will have range, but not depth. Either way, taking a closer look at how filters function should improve the impact of your words.

As we've seen, communication doesn't happen in a vacuum. No conversation is a true monologue. The listener—and what's going through their head and heart as they process what you say—plays a key role. Your listener is an active participant in the communication process. They are first-responders.

Your reader wears filters. You can learn how they work. You can go deep, or you can go wide. Either way, you can write to be read and speak to be heard on a new level.

YOUR READER'S FILTERS AT WORK

FILTERING THE MESSAGE

Most of us appreciate when someone pays attention to what we say. We generally speak to be heard. Yet, we know there's a dynamic at play that can distort this simple exchange, including between the writer and the reader. Our communication is informed by what everyone brings to the page, including how we filter words.

Like arrows shot from a bow, words do not fly in straight, uninterrupted lines. Everything from the weather, to physics, to unaccountable obstacles plays a part. Unless we account for what we can, our words have little hope of reaching their target.

Our listener's filters play a huge role in how our words are received or fall short of their intended. Although, it's important to say, filters are not the enemy. They serve a vital role. We don't communicate in a vacuum, and that's a good thing. It means the act of communication is subjective, personal and dynamic. Our words have meaning and significance. It is a great thing to be heard or read by someone who appreciates what we say.

Could a greater miracle take place
than for us to look through each
other's eyes for an instant?
Henry David Thoreau, Walden

Filters ensure the reader is respected and involved as a full-on participant, not a passive receptacle. All of us control our own communication processes. Each reader keeps watch. They decide what to tune in and what to pass by. No one can speak to another person in a meaningful way without their permission; without aligning with and/or accommodating their filters.

Taken further, filters serve to preserve the inner sanctum of the reader, who may otherwise be found vulnerable to a masterful (or manipulative or domineering or deceptive) communicator. Words have power. Filters ensure they don't have absolute power. Arrows do not fly through vacuums. Not in this world.

Filters serve to manage the communication process. They act as gatekeepers, ensuring respect and even safety.

Because filtering the message is the job of your reader, it's your job to be proactive. To respect their filters. To know your words are passing through guarded gates, being weighed as acceptable or otherwise. The whole time you're speaking, your listener is at work processing what you say. They are working to interpret and synthesize your words or preserve their right to ignore you. When we complain about being misunderstood, it's often because we failed to respect our listener's filters. Good communication goes two ways.

Words are relational.

Each type of reader has their own particular set of filters. These filters are meant to serve them well, and reinforce their place in the world, to help them do the work they are called to do. They deserve respect.

As we've seen, knowledge-hungry Scholars read people they trust and find credible. Community-nurturing Connectors read people who can relate. Mission-minded Agents listen for passion. Adventurers hear people who speak from the mountaintops they seek to conquer themselves. And mindful, gentle words are most likely to reach the ears of a Mystic.

Each reader's filters serve to preserve
and strengthen who they are.

Each type, of course, represents any number of actual people. The types are only categories and therefore don't cover every circumstance. Ultimately, individuals make their own decisions about what to read—or not—for their own reasons. But knowing how the types generally function, recognizing the patterns, is helpful—at least in pointing the arrow in the right direction, at the best angle. There are many ways to be proactive in how we seek to communicate and reach our reader. At the same time, who can account for the wind?

A word aptly spoken is like apples of
gold in settings of silver.
Proverbs 25:11

THE SCHOLAR'S FILTERS at work

The Scholar's filters work to gatekeep according to their desire to build knowledge in the world. This means they are open to material that runs along a serious vein, at least initially. If you don't take yourself seriously, neither can they. This doesn't mean they don't have a great sense of humour: they do. But it does mean they have fun mulling over serious ideas and problems. Intellectual stimulus is high on their list and is often the first gatekeeping requirement.

What does it mean to take yourself seriously, when seeking to communicate with a Scholar? It means you give credit where credit is due. The Scholar needs to know you know that knowledge is the work of many hands. To take yourself seriously, means you appreciate the efforts of those who have come before.

This doesn't mean you need formal credentials to speak to the Scholar, but you do have to be vested in your topic and/or established in your field. You have to say what you mean and mean what you say, if you hope to navigate the Scholar's filters. This reader values their mental energy and, above all, their integrity. They won't squander these inner resources.

"Can I trust the source?" is what the Scholar is asking themselves. "Is what you're saying worth my time?" It sounds harsh, perhaps, but not if you're a scholarly type. This reader makes no apologies for setting high the bar.

The Scholar values meaningful dialogue. They will seek to contribute to any conversation they find stimulating and rich with possibility. They're not total snobs.

Once a Scholar commits,
they commit.

The Scholar can be described as one of the most devoted readers of the five types. They are selective in their reading choices, but they're also students at heart. They want to learn, to know more, to engage in the Socratic process of growing together by asking timely, open-ended questions and sitting with the question until the answer proves satisfactory. Although, while they love to wrestle with the details, they're loath to expose their more playful, inventive side to anyone who doesn't really appreciate what they have to offer, what they bring to the table. At no point does communication cease to be a two-way street for this reader.

This reader can handle a lot. They have a large intellectual capacity that more ground-level writers can find daunting or even intimidating. If big words, research and complex layering isn't your thing, this is probably not your reader. On the other hand, once you've established a rapport with this type and understand how their filters work, the only limit on where you might go, is your imagination.

Scholars have a wide range of interests.

They find geography, history, culture, food, art and psychology as interesting as any other subject. They love to read about life, but also to physically journey. It's a rare Scholar without a stash of maps, worldly collections and a stand-by travel plan. They learn by reading, but also by doing, going and trying. If you have a personal experience to share and are able to embed it within a broader context, the Scholar will want to hear about it.

A food writer might write about farm produce and touch on water issues. A children's writer might dive into brain science. A memoirist might explore pioneer life. A scientist about a subject's responses according to the time of day—how psychology affects physiology. This reader responds to writers who connect the dots, who map the world in new ways.

Cross-pollination of ideas, events and facts is appreciated. Any new way to map the world exciting.

The Scholar believes in the educated imagination, the informed intellect, the communication process as dynamic interplay. Possibilities, for a Scholar, really are endless.

The Scholar works with ideas and ideals. They are constantly gathering up bits of know-how and extending unanswered questions, unsolved problems outwards... mulling over solutions, pondering possibilities. This means distracting, meandering, chatty conversation is something they actively tune out. While their interests are wide and intellect strong, they also need times of intense focus, to maintain mental clarity, which is their strength.

Times of pausing, retreats into solitude and even prolonged periods of silence may characterize this type of reader. They follow the proverb that iron sharpens iron. They like to be found sharp when hearing what you say and be able to return the favour. This type prefers to play to their strengths and hates to be found wanting.

When they do find themselves in unfamiliar territory, intellectually, reticence is their first response. They will hold back until they feel they have some grasp of what you're saying, and what they have to offer in return. This type doesn't use words as filler and won't fudge what they don't know. They are knowledge builders, which means they seek solid ground, each step of the way.

This means healthy, reciprocal, dynamic communication plays a vital role in their life and work. Writers and speakers with a fresh take and an active mind are well placed to connect with the Scholar.

A SOCIAL CONNECTOR'S FILTERS at work

A Social Connector knows what it means to stay in touch. And what it means to lose touch. This reader is listening for familiar voices, stories, words and sounds that signal home. It sounds simple, but the Connector understands that staying in touch is what holds most people together. They know when we lose touch with each other is when things can unravel…

In their chatty updates, they practice the maintenance-side of relationships. They check up on people. Keeping up-to-date with whatever concerns them. They like to have one finger on the pulse of their community, alert to its health and wellness. If what you say speaks to the concerns and heartbeat of their community, the Social Connector is a receptive listener. But they will tune out anything too far beyond the pale.

For this reader, stories build community, keeping it strong and connected. Stories remind us what it means to be human, to laugh, to share the burden and lighten each other's load. No one can fully appreciate a story unless they're willing to enter in to the subject's drama, to experience the same. This is what it means to feel empathy. And the Social Connector knows empathy as the lifeblood of any vital community.

Connectors connect through stories,
especially the ones that bring us
home to ourselves and others.

Narrative forms that house empathy and human drama speak strongly to this reader. They love a good story told well, with feeling.

This reader doesn't need to look further than their own life for examples of pressing human drama. This means stories that speak to their situation and circumstance are received as welcome friends. If what you say helps this reader navigate their own life better, their filters will swing wide open to you.

Connectors are not overly inward-looking. They tend to look to others, to the community as a source of peace and strength, rather than to themselves alone. The Connector knows the dangers of isolation; they are willing to listen to others as part of their own decision-making process, easily incorporating friendly, familiar voices into their own life journey. They are happy to read a book to hear what someone else is going through and might've gleaned along the way. They will listen intently to a speaker who speaks to them. They'll talk to a friend. Their world is an inclusive, expanding circle. Life is social.

Friends are the witnesses to our life.
David Whyte, poet

Because this reader looks to others to share the load, they understand that people come with problems. And that few of us are looking for the quick-fix. We'd rather be heard, understood and feel empathy.

Connectors value companionship. They are loath to treat problems as intruders to immediately resist and push out. They seek to embrace people holistically, which includes sitting with their problems, even befriending them. By lending a listening ear, they offer real support, not quick-fix solutions. Friendship itself goes a long way as help.

The month I spent apart from Jessica was eye-opening for me...without Jessica there to help me I felt lost and alone. Zoe Knightly, Chicken Soup for the Soul

This means you need speak from within the circle, for the benefit of all, to be heard. That first gatekeeping question, "Can you relate?" shows up throughout any sustained communication with a Connector.

Connectors understand that people come with problems; for them that's the strength of community: sharing the load. Easing the burden.

Connectors don't speak the language of overcoming, but enduring. Narrative rich with experience and shared struggles speaks to this reader. The details matter. As they would to any friend. The closer to home you bring the story, the better. This is not a selective reader. They're not impatient, waiting for you to get to the point. The point, for them, is in hearing your voice. Sharing your story. Hearing you and nurturing the circle in the process.

When someone feels heard, the Connector knows that person feel loved. Understood and accepted. These good feelings are the building blocks of their community.

The shape and structure of the story doesn't matter as much as the voice and tone. Life is not a cleanly edited document. It's a patchwork quilt of yellow sticky notes on the kitchen wall. Stories overlap, meander and often grow thanks to interruption, even disruption. The real-life nature of a story—its repeated phrases, its built-in drama— provides comfort to the circle of friends gathered to hear it, in part or in whole. Stories told in an imperfect way, or with a faltering voice, are easily enmeshed into the life of a Connector. They embrace those who can relate and who know the power of story.

It's good to hear your voice...
Sherry Waugh, a lifelong friend

If empathy for the human condition is at the heart of what you share, the Connector is your reader. They are the ones listening most closely for words of encouragement, understanding and kinship.

Nothing opens people up like an
encouraging word.

This reader does not embrace gloom and doom. They are realists, but they know life as a romance full of commitment and hope, not a tragedy marked with absurdity or farce. They have trouble enough of their own; they do not seek to borrow from others. This means they tend to read what leaves them feeling stronger, poised and more confident. They don't stick long with words that leave them feeling vaguely depressed, burdened or even useless.

This reader understands the world and its needs from a deep relational point of view. Their ability to connect with people and their problems—and skillfully work a room—makes this reader attractive and warm, someone others are anxious to meet and greet, to have a word with.

THE CHANGE AGENT'S FILTERS at work

The Change Agent is on a mission. They are open to hearing about opportunities to help those who cannot help themselves. Their mission field may be close to home and quite localized or broad and even global. The Change Agent will apply their talents for transformation to whatever project comes their way.

Their filters are receptive to anything that might equip them to do good work better. Of the five types, they are the most receptive to the language of persuasion, promotion and action-taking. Where the Connector is all about empathy and close conversation, the Change Agent is looking to get a job done and keen to talk about results. For this reader, stories aren't irrelevant, but they should have a point that helps move things forward.

> *(Thomas) Jefferson was devoted to the ideal of improving mankind but had comparatively little interest in people in particular...*
> *David McCullough,* John Adams

This passion for change can range from adopting new healthy habits, to promoting productivity by an NGO, to tackling social justice issues or exploring the overlap between faith and environmentalism. This reader appreciates being informed, up-to-date and generally being headed in the right direction, regardless of the topic at hand.

Where the Connector is content to sit with people and listen to their problems, the Change Agent starts to vibrate when engaging with someone who is stuck and who seems to want to stay stuck. The Change Agent doesn't offer empathy; they bring energy, drive and vision to the table. They seek to empower and be empowered.

Often an intense personality, they stand opposed to Status Quo on almost every level: personal, professional, social or societal. The Change Agent does not know what it means to confront a problem without trying to fix it. How to make the world a better place is their personal obsession.

While intense and sometimes impatient, this reader is deeply motivated to serve; to put their talents to good use. To make a difference for people who need good things to happen in practical ways.

The Change Agent is more than a fixer. They are a force.

There are few "inconvenient truths" in this reader's mind. If what you say has real-world application for the problems they are trying to solve, they do not remain passive, cool and detached. They hear you as someone who might help them make a difference. This makes for an active, attentive listener.

Their sense of urgency, combined with an intellect and energy committed to seeing success, means bullet points work well for this reader. Charts. Presentations. Argument. Logic impassioned for change and informed by compassion.

And when they commit, they see things through. They are reliable people to have onside. They long for a sense of completion in the world, to witness wholeness, and so give of themselves sacrificially. This means words around self-care, rest, time-management and resource-allocation are also welcome in this reader's world.

For them, life is not a journey blessed with an air of congeniality; it's a life and death proposition. Suffering knows no bounds and the battle has no real end goal. This means they tend to gravitate to writers and speakers who cast the world in black and white. Words that cut through clutter, cut to the chase and clear a path to success.

For the Change Agent, time is of the essence. As a matter of course, they are in a hurry, on their way out the door or have only a moment to spare. This means they listen with one ear on you and the other pressed to the ground, ready to move on a moment's notice towards what calls them.

This makes for an exacting reader, but it also means the language of team works well. They are big picture thinkers who know no job worth doing can be done alone. The Change Agent is aware of their own limitations and pressed attitude towards others and time. They know their need to be on team. This felt need makes them quick to trust others' competency; as much as they like to be empowered, they believe in empowering others. They're aware they're only half-present at any one time, choosing to be in two or more places, constantly in motion, advancing the cause.

This reader recognizes that one person can't do it all. It's the rare Change Agent that sees themselves as a one-man or one-woman show. This reader truly values team effort. Because they're on mission to serve people, they're committed to working with people to make that happen. This reader is not a theorist. They are not an observer. They are action and results-oriented with a strong pragmatic sense of what it takes to realize ideals within real-world settings. They know they're not perfect and are open to compromising with others to make good things happen—sooner than later. Subtlety and suggestion often fall short with this reader. They want to know how to get the job done.

Being on mission,
means being on team.

Just like this reader is not a heavy-handed task master; neither will they respond to the language of shame or blame. They respond to the language of praise and affirmation. "Good job, everyone."

This positive get-the-job-done attitude means they are open to the strong, hope-filled language of persuasion, but not to strong-arm techniques or pressure tactics. Although, if what you say aligns with the work they feel called to, you can speak as long and loud as you like. You can even shout. Volume is not at issue for this reader.

The Change Agent is open to anyone who can empower them to do what they need to do; fulfill their mandate, answer their call or serve their part. They're just as open to hearing what you say about rest, relaxation and personal restoration, mercy and inner healing. After all the hours they invest improving the lives of others, they can easily find themselves in need of some tender loving care. There are two sides to this reader: the one that seeks to be empowered, mobilized and inspired. And the side that needs to retreat, refuel and re-evaluate. Although, while the topics may occupy different ends of the spectrum (activity/rest), both sides of this reader respond to strong, hope-filled, forward-thinking and moving language. Empowerment is the overarching theme for this reader.

If this is your reader, your words will bring life and will be multiplied by the sheer force of this reader's personality, not to mention their professional influence. If the Change Agent likes what you say, they're bound to pass it on. If this is your ideal reader, your words are likely to make a real difference in someone's world.

THE ADVENTURER'S FILTERS at work

This reader's filters work to keep the dream alive.

Life is best lived, and perhaps only lived, as an adventure. This type is seeking to be immersed in a believable world where stakes are high and people three-dimensional. For them to enter in to what you say, there must be a situation that calls for courage. A mountain to climb, a river to run or someone to befriend in a practical way.

Their filters are attuned to personal calls to action, especially on behalf of people they care about. They are not on a mission to change the world, only give it their personal best. The Adventurer is not about improving society through a team effort, but about reaching the summit on their own steam and having someone onside to prize the view.

The Adventurer does not sit with people and their problems. They work to overcome. To take on life's challenge of really living. They seek to lead inspiring lives. They read to see people living this dream; to bear witness to overcoming. They look for examples to follow. This means they respond to language that is visual and visceral.

They respond to concrete challenges; opportunities to dig deeper, climb higher. They want a clear picture of the situation, to gauge the stakes. This reader does not speak the language of waiting and learning, but of sacrifice and daring. Of action and risk-taking.

While the Adventurer trusts their instinct to read a situation and react, they're also prepared. They do their homework. Think through logistics. Assess risk and count cost. They know the paralyzing effect of fear and uncertainty, the danger of being caught half-ready. They look ahead and plan accordingly. The technical side of a climb is as much as part of the adventure as your choice of companions. At the same time, they keep one eye on the summit and are willing to set forth despite potential setbacks. It's like they've caught the scent of glory.

This can-do attitude means they are ready to move on a dime, at the slightest provocation or invitation. Not because they're impulsive, but because they are in a constant state of readiness; they read widely and store up everything they learn by reading and listening to those who have gone before them and succeeded. They are steeped in the language and story of overcoming. Mentally and emotionally, their bags are packed. They are ready to go.

Simply point an Adventurer to a summit and be prepared to be taken aback by their supply of courage and know-how. They know that to summit requires all of them, 100 per cent not 99.

They expect the same kind of all-in competency and super-tight structuring in storytelling from those they read. To detach or withdraw is a failure to commit, which can be costly when it comes to reaching the summit; summits belong to people who give their all, not to those doling out half-measures or holding back a piece of themselves. Summits take courage which requires commitment. This is the standard this reader holds themselves to, and the one they apply to would-be communicators and storytellers.

The Adventurer wants to be immersed, to deep-dive, to trust the storyteller as a master of their craft. The Connector will listen for voice, humour, cadence and tone, but for the Adventurer, structure is core because it means there's a plan; it means the story is leading somewhere and has a good chance of reaching the summit. Success is in sight.

Where the Change Agent needs to feel empowered by your words, the Adventurer needs to feel equipped. Where the Agent needs to feel inspired to stay on task, the Adventurer needs to be motivated to begin.

This reader responds to the language of immediacy; action and responsibility; of consequence and significance. To reach this reader, raise the stakes, turn on the heat, point to the problem and equip them to succeed. Demonstrate. Illustrate. Story-tell. Do not teach, theorize, banter or draw a chart. Speak of human problems that can only be resolved by superhuman effort and ingenuity, with extraordinary courage by real-world heroics.

Whether they're helping someone through a bad health report, messed up relationship, or accompanying them on a spiritual quest, the Adventurer knows confidence begets confidence. And nothing builds a person's confidence like success.

*The babe in the cradle knows about
the dragon. He needs stories to know
about St. George.*
G.K. Chesterton, theologian & writer

There is almost nothing that will stop an Adventurer from giving their best, for a chance at reaching the summit and helping others do the same.

*Defeat. Failure. These words are not
in their vocabulary.*

The Adventurer wants to spread the glory. To instill a hunger for the summit in lives circumscribed by shadows. At their best, an Adventurer wants to break through the darkness and usher in the light.

This can happen in simple, ordinary ways. Like helping a friend navigate life's transitions. Or win back a lover or connect with a child. Or it can happen in spectacular ways, like climbing a mountain, traversing cross-continent or collaborating on a cookoff.

Whatever the challenge, this type responds to voices that speak from a place of experience, not entitlement or enchantment. They know if you've seen all you claim to have seen. Done what you said you did. This reader has that discerning sixth sense.

THE MYSTIC 'S FILTERS at work

Mystics live their own truth.

This reader seeks words that align with their love and knowledge of truth. Words that lead them deeper. This reader is not listening for information or personal connection. They are not scanning the screen to learn more or reading to be entertained or even engaged. They are simply and only listening for truth that resonates with their spirit. They attune to what hits the mark and pass over what falls short.

This makes for interesting work from the writer's perspective or for speakers hoping to wow the Mystics in the room. This reader looks for the meaning behind words. They listen for what might be suggested in the tone. They want the backstory, not the story. This can make a potential storyteller wonder what to say next.

Would-be communicators need to know this type of reader is essentially spiritual in outlook and sensibility. Unless you come with kindness, they will struggle to receive what you say. Before they can hear you, their spirits must sense you come in the name of truth and love.

This reader knows words have power. That words can cultivate peace, hope and joy. Or, they can stoke regret, anger and despair. Words can leave their mark on a soul. The Mystic is particularly sensitive to this and works to guard their heart. Spiritual self-care is key.

For a Mystic, words that come from the centre of a person can also serve as a bridge between spirit and flesh, heaven and earth, idea and friend. The Mystic lives very close to this bridge between heaven and earth, thought and matter. In some ways, they are its guardians, its keepers.

Once their interest is piqued, the Mystic doesn't need a lot of words or lengthy discourse to establish common ground with you, as long as you're speaking the same language as them. The most important thing to a Mystic, when you speak, is to understand your meaning.

While content is important, so is breathing space to process meaning. This means, as a writer or speaker, if you prefer the language of the classroom, board room or city commute, your words may meet with deaf ears.

For a Mystic, the root word of communication is very much communion.

This is why Mystics are radically selective about what they read or listen to in a deep way.

A Mystic can read one sentence and be lost in thought for an hour—if it resonates with them.

While all five types listen for authenticity—what rings true to them and has meaning according to their lights—the Mystic is the most unapologetic for this self-care approach.

This reader has no qualms about asking the question: "Does it ring true for me?"

Like all five types of readers, the Mystic is seeking, in their own way and within their own context, the unmistakable note of authenticity.

To reach this reader, you can be subtle, poetic or abstract. Suggestive, nuanced or uber-clear. But what you say must be informed by your own spiritual journey and desire to live from the inside out, with faith in the unseen but ever present. You must share a sense of God's truth and love to reach this reader in a deep way.

For them, reading is a spiritual act, part of the reflective process and a means of communicating on a deeper level than casual conversation allows.

This reader is not on an adventure. They are not looking, primarily, to change the world or even make it a better place. They're not looking to fit in with the crowd, or to make friends. They're not interested in learning something new if it doesn't resonate and align with what's going on for them, spiritually. As Trappist monk and author, Thomas Merton, puts it in *Thoughts in Solitude*, "As far as the writer [Merton] is concerned, there was no adventure to write about, and if there had been, it would not have been confided to paper in any case. These are simply thoughts on the contemplative life, fundamental intuitions which seemed, at the time, to have a basic importance."

As a result, reading material for this reader can vary widely, although a few common themes tend to emerge. It can be the state of a soul, or the effect of chronic pain on a body. It may the beauty of a natural landscape or the plight of an endangered species. It can be the desire for immortality hinted at in a happy life or perfect love. Whatever the topic, this reader consistently brings a heightened awareness to the human condition and longing for the divine. They love to see below the surface and bring to the light any glimmers of eternity, hope and spiritual sustenance they are able to receive.

It's through this attentive, prayerful approach to life that they seek to shore up faith in the world, to bless others by living with the integrity of a fellow pilgrim and world-weary traveller. By being true to their own calling and growing into their spiritual identity, they believe their own lives will naturally serve as a witness to God's larger reality, plan, love and concern for people everywhere. By being true, they allow themselves to be seen as living examples of perfect, eternal truth embodied in imperfect, transitory flesh and blood. They become the bridges that they spend their life traversing.

*A mystical experience is one in which
there is no direct causation within the
spatio-temporal universe.*
Michael Casey, Strangers to the City

In the end, a Mystic owns their language choice and all its
implications. This reader thrives on symbols and
metaphors, word pictures and spiritual insights. They seek
to grow faith in the world, usually starting and ending
with their own. Anyone seeking to communicate and
commune with this reader understands those two words
mean the same thing and carry the equal weight. And is
willing to become a bridge-builder.

HOW TO REACH YOUR READER

The SCHOLAR's checklist

✓ Scholars are builders of knowledge. DO YOUR HOMEWORK. And then share your passion. To reach the people wearing the Scholar's filter you'll need to back up what you're saying with facts and figures. You also need to have some context around those facts; they can't float.

✓ Pair respect for the intellect with AWE for the power of the imagination, which plays such an important part in knowledge building.

✓ DEEP DIVE ON YOUR TOPIC. Once you've done your homework, demonstrate mastery to engage the Scholar in an active and dynamic way. Scholars are builders. They need to contribute.

✓ BRING TOGETHER MULTIPLE VOICES. Cross-pollinate ideas. Then challenge perspectives. Don't be afraid to take risks.

✓ Once you prove yourself an expert, DO NOT FEAR THE MAZE of unanswered questions or possibilities. Explore. Scholars don't need all the answers and rhetorical questions aren't usually appreciated. Don't be afraid to peer over the edge of the abyss and wonder... Scholars are often student-philosophers at heart.

✓ Because the Scholar is a student before they are a teacher, learning something new is vital to holding their attention. ENTERTAIN AND ENLIGHTEN, BUT MOST OF ALL EDUCATE. If learning is not a priority for you, this is not your ideal reader.

✓ LEAVE YOUR READER SPACE to enter in to what you have to say. Their ideal setting is *not* the monologue-heavy classroom or take-away conference model. They do their best thinking in open spaces free of external constraints, such as bells, timers, crowds, noise and shallow distraction. Take a leisurely, unhurried approach.

✓ Don't lose momentum. Don't repeat yourself. To fully engage a Scholar, you cannot be a lazy editor of your own information. MINE AND POLISH THE DNA of what you say before you say it.

✓ CREDIT YOUR SOURCES. Formally thank them. Whether it's personal or professional, good communication with a Scholar is marked by respect and consideration. Formalism often equates to trustworthiness for this reader.

✓ HONOUR THEIR WISDOM. Scholars are often the supporting genius behind creative undertakings and/or significant breakthroughs.

The SOCIAL CONNECTOR's checklist

✓ To reach this reader, empathize with personal problems, ones we all share. Be AUTHENTIC.

✓ RELATE THROUGH DIALOGUE. Give voice. Before a Social Connector opts to go deeper they put out trusty feelers, asking themselves, "Is this familiar? Can I relate? Is it relevant to my life and circumstance?" If the answers are a resounding yes, the Connector is open to hearing more. If you don't have a knack for dialogue and embellished storytelling, you probably don't have the ear of a Social Connector, who has an unerring ear for true-to-life dialogue. If what you say lacks an ear for how people talk, or your dialogue tends to be clunky or judgmental, this is not your best listener.

✓ To stay real is no small task, as the Connector knows. In a world full of fragmentation, the connective power and holistic feel of the circle offers a restorative, revitalizing and hope-filled refuge for many people. STAY REAL.

✓ Keep it honest and HUMBLE. Where the Scholar needs you to play with your material, exhibiting mastery and mindfulness, the Social Connector needs to see you downplay ego. For the Scholar, a healthy ego is a sign of a healthy mind. For the Social Connector boasting is taboo, breaking

sacred bonds of affirmation, acceptance and
inclusivity that define the circle.

✓ TELL GOOD STORIES. Use believable
dialogue, clearly described settings and vulnerable,
relational drama. Relational storytelling is key
because faces and voices recreate life at home,
which is a core value for this reader.

✓ A natural multi-tasker and competent project
manager, the Connector is responsible to many
people. BE HIGHLY RELEVANT. Speak from
within the circle, not outside. Connectors are the
hub of their circle. Their lives are not organized
around information and knowledge like the
Scholar's. Their life is a circle; it revolves around
familiar people, activities and issues we all share.

✓ This reader believes in giving other people space
to work things through, while still providing
empathy. Empathize. DO NOT JUDGE. The
Social Connector's high level of competency and
social awareness makes them the ideal candidate
to be a problem solver. But, they respect people's
need to journey, to fully enter in and experience
the setting and drama of their own life.

✓ CONNECT. Create points of entry and feedback.
A Connector needs opportunity to respond to
you. This need is not shared by the other four
types of readers. Only a Connector *needs* to have a

say, offer a response, fill out an evaluation form, or put a review online.

✓ DO NOT FIX. Celebrate Multi-Tasking Jugglers and Air-Traffic Control Personnel. A Social Connector can easily do three, four, or 15 things on the run. They will manage the needs of a large family, business, project or group with aplomb. This talent for multi-tasking people, projects and problems, means they live on the move. It's hardly worthwhile trying to slow this reader down or speak the language of rest and retreat.

✓ Stories revolve around people and their problems. ASSUME THE BEST OF PEOPLE. The best stories have no (obvious) moral tale. Stories reinforce and celebrate the personal side of life; they incorporate the messy side. As any good story demonstrates, people do not live in pristine, sterile environments for long. The average person can be rude and inconsistent. And, they can be far more noble and self-sacrificing, truth-seeking and loving and committed than we imagine. Stories are about unpacking the neat and tidy versions of reality we tell each other and finding out that where people really live is much more interesting and life-giving, not to mention entertaining, tragic and strange. Stories are the primary way people connect and bond because they're what keep us honest. Stories are windows into another person's world, and Connectors feel very privileged when offered a glimpse into someone else's life.

✓ BE POSITIVELY ENTERTAINING! Embellish at will. Gossip can be good. Being left out of the loop, overlooked or sidelined in a conversational thread is tantamount to a relational breakdown for a Connector. They need to be informed, current and relevant. The Connector seeks out and promotes the familiar through harmless storytelling, personal sharing and disjointed bits of gossip and FYIs.

✓ Home is a guiding metaphor for the Social Connector. BLESS THE HOME. Even when they find themselves somewhere completely new and hugely public, they still try to make everyone feel at home, to extend that familiar feeling of love and acceptance. This is their power. They see the world through a friendly, communal lens.

✓ SPEAK TO THE HEART. Embrace its language and vocabulary. With a communal outlook on life, the Connector tends to take responsibility for the emotional temperature and tone of an interaction.

✓ DON'T DISCOUNT PERFECTIONISM. The Connector is not a controlling personality, or a perfectionist. They are happiest with arms extended in several directions, fostering the flow of people and activity. The circle is open, there's always room for one more chair at the table. In this way, the language of how to make things better in their own world, for the people they care about, speaks straight to their heart.

✓ ENCOURAGE. Work on happy endings. This tends to make everyone feel better, which encourages others to look up and reach out, expanding the circle rather than closing it.

✓ OFFER PRACTICAL SUPPORT. Provide strong, warm emotional frameworks. Ideally you are open and willing to share your personal story with the Connector, willing to honour the oral traditions of community building, rather than knowledge building. You're in touch with your own feelings and understand appropriate, two-way give-and-take.

✓ The wisdom of the Social Connector lies in the paradox between their ability to multitask a large number of projects, and at the same time resist the urge to solve people's problems. HONOUR THEIR WISDOM. A Social Connector may be easily distracted. While they are there to listen long, they are not there to fix the problem. In this caring enough not to fix you, the Social Connector demonstrates the wisdom of the pastoral role. Extending hospitality, coming alongside and attempting to understand others; asking good questions and sharing the details of life openly and without condemnation is one of the Connector's great charms.

The CHANGE AGENT's checklist

✓ An invitation to engage doesn't have to be personal for the Agent to respond strongly; it has to be passionate. To reach this reader, simply cut to the chase, clear a path forward and then… make way. DEMONSTRATE THE WAY FORWARD. The Change Agent is results-driven. This means bullet point presentations are just fine. Short books or seamless presentations are welcome. Visuals charts and diagrams are great. The Change Agent has a huge capacity to synthesize information.

✓ STAY POSITIVE. Identify the problem, but then help clear the obstacles. There is nothing more discouraging to a Change Agent than to feel progress is not being made.

✓ This reader is a citizen of a world with a strong sense of roles and responsibilities within their sphere of influence. THINK BIG.

✓ DO NOT ACCEPT STATUS QUO. Get angry. Change Agents want to be empowered and inspired to do good work, this side of heaven. Their motivation is usually good, their talent high and judgment sound. It's okay to call a spade a spade and at times, get angry.

✓ FOCUS on solutions. The Change Agent needs to be on-task. While this task-focus is different from the Social Connector's people-focus, both readers ultimately work to strengthen and uphold the people-issues they care about. The difference is: The Change Agent needs to be working towards solving the problem, whereas the Connector is content to sit with it. The Agent is usually on mission. This disruptive quality is, of course, anathema to the Connector's sense of group harmony and personal peacekeeping, but the Agent won't rest until a solution is found.

✓ PERSUADE, but don't sell. You don't need to spell out the meaning and implications of what you say. This reader likes bite-size information pertaining directly to their cause, whatever helps them stay motivated—to keep caring.

✓ EMPOWER. Speak project management-ese. The Change Agent lives out of their passion to change the world. This reader is purpose-driven, not people-driven. If you can show a Change Agent how to do good work better, you have their undivided attention. Ideally you will also help them better organize their projects and people.

✓ The Change Agent does not enjoy becoming immersed in a believable world of human drama. DO NOT TELL STORIES WITHOUT A POINT. They are too concerned with the task at hand to dwell long below the surface or within the multi-faceted worlds that fiction explores and unpacks. Besides, they tend to have enough real-world drama in their own life. They are impatient with fictional or anecdotal accounts of what they experience every day.

✓ To inspire a Change Agent, paint a picture of progress in concrete, tangible terms. EMPLOY VERBS. Know the numbers. Use charts. Or put them in touch with people whose lives have improved as a result of their efforts. Signs of success and tangible results are to a Change Agent what cards and gifts are to a Social Connector, or what breakthroughs and insights are to a Scholar.

✓ Speak the language of inspiration, seek to activate and motivate. PAINT THE BIG PICTURE. They like to know how to overcome obstacles and reach goals, build team and find success, but they are mostly motivated by Big Picture language. Word pictures. Metaphors. Quantifiable ways to make a real difference in the world. Goals, not problems, speak to this reader. And the bigger the goal, the better.

✓ SPEAK TO CORE VALUES. Move mountains.

✓ MAKE IMPORTANT THINGS URGENT. This reader likes to be reminded of how to keep relationships and intangible, personal values on track as well. Although they're big picture people, they know the small things matter too; they just need to be reminded of this more than the other four types of readers. This reader appreciates bluntness that demonstrates respect for the reader's intention, motivation and character. They are do-gooders, which means they have a heart for getting things right—for doing the right thing by everyone as much as possible.

✓ DO NOT APOLOGIZE for strong language (which is different than being crude or rude).

✓ DO NOT DWELL ON PEOPLE'S PROBLEMS OR PAIN. The Change Agent is a fixer, unlike the Connector or the Scholar. This means they don't like to dwell on the problem or the pain. They'd rather put away the tea cups and get to work on the solution. This reader becomes very uncomfortable with too many personal details, drawing a clear line between public and private spheres. They don't wish to pry.

✓ DEMONSTRATE SELF-CARE. Affirm and applaud self-care, even while promoting team service and sacrificial giving. This reader is a radical. They appreciate anyone who can bring balance without losing sight of the goal or undermining the passion they wish to direct towards finding solutions.

✓ HONOUR THEIR WISDOM. It's about helping the disempowered. This reader has grit, guards their ego and is most receptive to strong language.

The ADVENTURER's checklist

✓ IMMERSE YOUR READER. Do not hold back. "Climb on," says the Adventurer. "You can do it. Here is the way. Follow me." The Adventurer is listening for a challenge to the best part of them, where courage seeks to rise.

✓ CREATE HIGHLY BELIEVABLE scenarios (fiction, fantasy or true-story). This type of reader has a huge appetite for story, but they don't suffer fools or amateurs lightly. You have to know your subject (on a first-hand, experiential basis) *and* be a master storyteller to reach an Adventurer.

✓ BE STRATEGICALLY SELECTIVE IN DETAILS. Stories with a physical element must have all of the I's dotted and T's crossed. The physical equipment and how and when it is used is a key part of the story for the Adventurer. They want to know what is required to succeed. How, exactly, to they handle this sticky situation or that worse-case scenario?

✓ Adventure should have a purpose, and often EMOTIONS ARE THE BEST PART. This reader has a large appetite for stories about overcoming. Stories packed with adventure and adrenaline; first-person description and eyewitness accounts speak to the Adventurer. Believability and selective detail, real life drama and surmounting insurmountable difficulties all work. At the same time, they need a purpose, a reason to risk, and more often that purpose has *a name*. A person to care about.

✓ MAKE IT ABOUT SAVING THE DAY. They are competent, informed, experienced and, most importantly, have courage to spare. This reader wants to be the hero—and often is to many people in their own life.

✓ Adventurers do not solve a problem as much as they attack it. BE SPECIFIC. FOCUS. Define scope. Be specific about what it means to conquer this mountain, fix that relationship. Define success in concrete, tangible, visceral terms. The higher the stakes, the better.

✓ Take risks. GET OUTSIDE. Someone reading through this lens is seeking to live life outside, and writ large.

✓ For this reader, there are no easy fixes. SUPERHEROES ARE BORING. Keep it real. People have to own their victory, earn the triumph and make it personal.

✓ TEST THE LIMITS of your characters, let their life's adventure be a lesson to others. Create compelling examples to follow. Genre is not the issue for this reader. Fictional worlds hold as much value as non-fiction tales. This reader is highly intuitive. They easily cross-reference. For them, life's lessons are true wherever they're found.

✓ LIVE FOR ADVENTURE, but don't forget to admire the view. The best conversations and sharpest insights are often found on top of mountains after a long climb up.

✓ This reader seeks to OVERCOME THEMSELVES as much as any mountain. They do not have to leave home to do this—although they thrive outside and in action—any vicarious adventure will speak to the core of who they are, and allow them to enter in.

✓ Where the Change Agent is on mission, requires a team and can measure progress in quantifiable ways, the Adventurer requires a vision, a grand vista and a friend. INVITE SOMEONE to come along. This reader is not on mission. They are seeking to come alongside someone in need. To overcome together.

✓ BELIEVE FOR THE BEST, as courage and trust go hand-in-hand. When communicating with an Adventurer, trust their integrity, their ability to root for good to triumph over evil. Steer clear from ambiguous endings, apathy and hard-to-crack cynicism. They don't need happy endings, but do need clarity, satisfaction and believability.

✓ TOUCH PEOPLE, be physical. Stay in contact, even when there's reason to be afraid. For the Adventurer the value lies in rising to a personal test, overcoming inner demons, and demonstrating trust and love in the face of nameless fears. This is not about being overly sensitive or sentimental, but it is about having a genuine sensibility, a deep appreciation of life's challenges. This is not about bravado. This is about overcoming universal challenges; the ones we all face with the same hopes and fears.

✓ BE KIND. Do not stereotype but avoid political correctness. Focus on humanity.

✓ Respect the mountain. Not everyone summits. Do not lower standards or demands for the sake of the majority. Whatever it takes to succeed and feel satisfied, is what it takes. The Adventurer's motto: NO EXCUSES. NO REGRETS.

✓ HONOUR THEIR WISDOM. The wisdom of the Adventurer is not one of empathy or empowerment or even deep intellectual engagement. The wisdom of this reader is hard won, either through experience or vicariously. Stagnation is one step away from real sickness, as far as the Adventurer is concerned. Their wisdom is often found in simply getting people moving: up the mountain, toward their goals and dreams.

The MYSTIC's checklist

✓ Mystics are the lighthouse keepers in a world at sea. The best way to reach this reader is to live deeply, TRUST GOD, be yourself, and let experience outstrip explanation.

✓ OWN YOUR VOICE. Are you naturally a casual or formal person? There is no 'right' answer, only a true one. This type of reader is highly intuitive (like the Adventurer), but their genius lies in discerning the unseen rather than the physical challenge at hand. The first thing they use to test the waters is the sound of your voice. It must be true. Ring authentic. Align with who you are.

✓ While the Mystic thrives on inner peace, deep rest and uninterrupted times of focus, they also love to engage with their work. VALUE SPIRITUAL LIFE WORK. The Mystic has no doubt the work they do, to own the truth, to live it inside and out has value. For them, it is vital—essential to maintaining the spiritual life of the world. While this is a long-held tradition from a monastic or even rabbinical perspective, today it may not be as well understood, but that doesn't mean that the age-old desire for unity with the divine as a means of bridging heaven and earth is any less alive among us. To reach this reader, see yourself as part of this work. Engage on a collegial level.

✓ KEEP TO THE MAIN. Mystics are discerning responders to life's questions and people's problems, but this quality takes a lot of time to develop and grow, making them jealous guardians of their own time. This reader has no trouble saying, "No," when it comes to keeping life simple and stress free, the calendar light and responsibilities in check.

✓ The Mystic is selective in their responses to go deeper in life, love or faith. The invitation to listen to what you say must resonate with something already alive and well within them. Deep must speak to deep. LIVE WHAT YOU PREACH. Know your truth.

✓ The Mystic resents straightforward pointers on how to grow spiritually. ABANDON INSTRUCTION. Promote wonder. The Mystic requires gaps to dwell in. Subtleties to flesh out. Prophetic utterances. The Mystic loves to read words the page can barely contain. To embody the word itself.

✓ REFLECT ON WHAT YOU'RE SAYING. Acknowledge the intimate link you have with your reader. Stay close to the page. Inhabit the words. Be self-aware without drawing attention to yourself. Serve the reader.

✓ The Mystic must be drawn with the gentlest of flames. SUGGEST, INTIMATE, WHISPER.

Their attention focuses when they catch that *flicker of light* in the dark. With the Mystic you can be oblique. The Mystic does not need the roadmap the Change Agent is looking for. They only need a glimmer, a flicker on the horizon to set off on their own journey of discovery.

✓ Wholesale immersion in their inner world can take them to remote places. As a result, they are a bit of a walking contradiction. In one moment closely attuned to what you are saying, yet largely remote in the next. LEAVE ROOM to wander, enter in and wander back out again. The Mystic values their freedom to come and go. They can be intimate and conversational *and* detached at the same time. Perceptive *and* clueless. Altogether, this makes them a thoughtful, attentive reader who, at any moment, may put down your book or close the screen. Tightly woven narratives don't work well for this reader, as they've likely forgotten or misplaced what they read before looking up, or walking away, before returning to the page… "Now, where were we?"

✓ STRIVE FOR BEAUTY of form, eloquence. The Mystic is averse to the powers of persuasion or groupthink or community buy-in. They are unlikely to be impressed with the latest body of research. And they tend not to immerse themselves in fiction. Words of truth, love and meaning shaped and delivered in beautiful forms speak to this reader. Think poetry, devotionals, essays and art or history books.

✓ METAPHORS house meaning. The language of metaphor and visualization, prophetic pictures, the artistic vision of unseen realms and the discernment of underlying currents within a room, doesn't lend itself to popular literature or social media connections. It lends itself to the pared down possessions of the pilgrim. To a few good books and images. The Mystic, like the Scholar, needs time alone and away to process, but they are not processing what they've heard or read of others' ideas. They are processing what they felt, overheard, seen or discerned in the spiritual realm. This kind of processing takes a lot of time, and, often, silence. The breathable language of metaphor serves their purpose well.

✓ For the Mystic to hear what you're saying it must resonate in a deep and soulful way. This is because they live what they know: they are theologically oriented. To lose the ear of a Mystic, simply start going over your To-Do list for the week, or expound on your three-year plan, or the latest on home organization, or the best-selling anything. These are not less-than topics, they simply fail to register on the radar for the Mystic, attuned to the INEFFABLE SIDE OF LIFE.

✓ For the Mystic, the truth is alive and well. It is living and breathing. It is organic and growing.

It's relational and dynamic. The Mystic understands that to reach the summit of a mountain there is no straight line. The path often zigzags. And each turn is worth seeing, offering its own vantage point. TRUST THE READER. Shake the urge to overtly mentor or guide.

✓ SIMPLICITY, simplicity, simplicity. They actively seek to keep the lines of communication open between their spirit and the Holy Spirit. The Mystic is seeking revelation from God. This means the practical side of what you say must be kept to a dull roar for the Mystic to maintain the quiet posture of listening that they find so essential to their way of life.

✓ The wisdom of the Mystic is found in their startling capacity to be bored. HONOUR THEIR WISDOM. They are the ones most willing to wait for inspiration and endure prolonged periods of darkness or silence in order to be found aligned with and receptive to the light, when revelation does pierce the clouds. Much like the Scholar is willing to work for an intellectual breakthrough, or the Change Agent a breakthrough on the social justice front, or the Adventurer on the personal and physical front, the Mystic knows spiritual breakthroughs come at a cost—and is willing to put in the time to see it happen.

CONCLUSION

WE CAN ALL REACH SOMEONE on a deep level with our words. Words are meant to be heard. Yet, we all hear each other through our own particular set of lenses, or filters.

Thankfully, these filters can be better known, more fully accommodated and basically less feared. When someone fails to hear us, or read what we write, it's not a personal rejection or slight (necessarily). It's more often a simple failure to hear. We spoke. They listened; but our words did not get past their filters. Did not resonate. We failed to speak their language. And that's okay, as long as we stayed true to our own language and made the best effort we could. But nine times out of the proverbial ten, communication does take work. And ten out of ten, it's worth the effort. To be heard is a beautiful thing.

But, before we can be heard, we often need to listen to our listener. To hear the click and whirl of our would-be hearer's filters at work. We need to seek to understand before being understood, to borrow the words of a saint known for listening to the quietest but most universal speech: the birds, the Spirit and the heart of Man.

Francis of Assisi knew what it meant to hear and be heard; to be in deep fellowship; to walk together as one. We don't all seek this level of communion in our own lives or through our livelihoods as aspiring communicators, but it's a great picture of what's possible: of the life of words breaking through clouds, of what it means to get to the heart of a matter, to be transformed, even exalted. To humbly receive a word planted within.

Ideally, you've read and heard what I had to say, in my attempt to share a sliver of understanding on this vital topic of communication: one that really does run the gamut from the mundane to the mystical. Ideally, you've been able to identify with the Scholar as one seeking to build knowledge; or the Social Connector as one seeking to companion; or the Change Agent who's generally on mission; or the Adventurer, always open to the next challenge or the Mystic dwelling quietly on their own terms. At least one type of reader, if not more, may have resonated with you, as a writer, a fellow-reader and as a listener in the context of your life.

As you probably noticed, all five types are most easily reached by someone who shares their key questions, core needs and basic outlooks. A Scholar is most easily reached by a Scholar and a Change Agent by a Change Agent. This is true for all types.

If, however, you're someone who needs to reach a diverse audience, then consider opening up the podium or pulpit, the stage or the platform to other voices, other types. Work in team. Diversify the voices speaking to match the variety of people listening. People can't change their filters, or the way they hear your words. It's very difficult for a listener to adjust the way they hear. It's much easier for a communicator to tailor their words, since they're the initiator of the interaction and, therefore, are in a position to be proactive, thoughtful and intentional. A listener has to adjust on the fly. Without the benefit of feedback or forethought.

There are many ways to improve how we listen, of course. But listening is a subjective act first. The listener is essentially in the position of *responder*. Once words are spoken, the train has left the station. It's up to the speaker to have made the plan, consider the best route and adjust their speed and approach. Pre-prepared communication is not ultimately subjective, it's objective and better suited to changes and tweaks. It's hard to think a train might leave its station without being given a once-over. Neither would a speech, article or book leave a writer's desk without multiple edits. This book is proposing one of those edits be done solely for the type of reader the writer has in mind.

To reach your reader, write with *your type* in mind. Speak their language. Make choices in light of their preferences. Answer their questions. Address their concerns. They may need to hear your credentials. Or they may need to know who you know. Or they may need to feel your passion or want to climb the mountain with you. Or, they may be seeking to live the truth of their own lives. These are five different types of readers. Each one requires a certain kind of filtering on your part. Their own edit. Their own personal consideration.

The onus is on you, the person aiming to be heard, to accommodate your various listener's filters.

One type of communicator cannot reach all five types of listeners easily or effectively. One type of writer cannot reach five readers in a meaningful way. We hear through our filters. We each need to have this accommodated in some way by anyone hoping to reach us with their words.

You may have recognized some cross-over between the types. In your own leisure-time reading you may be a critically-minded Scholar; but in your work as a writer, an impassioned Change Agent; and in your day-to-day speech a friendly Social Connector, asking after people's problems. This is natural. We are far more than any 'type.'

This is just as true for people who write and speak for a living. Our voice on the page, screen or stage is the voice of a distinct, living, breathing individual. We each have our own voice and we each hear in our own way. Being aware of the interplay between types and individuals is important. The types are meant as a helpful guide. Limited, but in many ways, indispensable.

This guide to the five filters of the five types of readers— the Scholar, Social Connector, Change Agent, Adventurer and Mystic—is an invitation to approach your would-be audience in a new way, and ultimately to take your words and communication forward. One listener at a time.

> *Communication is an art, but it's also work. The work of a committed soul hoping to reach another soul.*

ABOUT THE AUTHOR

Thanks for reading.

These observations, insights and revelations into how and why people read have been gleaned over the years and are informed by my work as a journalist, freelance writer, communications consultant, writing instructor and editor.

I've worked with words for more than 25 years, with the intent to strengthen understanding, persuade, connect or enlighten. This work has extended into a passion for leading creative workshops, hosting spiritual formation opportunities and writing poetry, that sparsest of forms.

I trust this book will help you reach others with your words, your thoughts, your ideas. Communication is all about sharing and growing together. Truly, we are meant to be heard—and understood on a deeper, more satisfying level.

www.daynawrites.com